HELEN HALL LIBRARY
City of League City
DISCARD
100 West Walker
League City, TX 77573-3899

D0601555

JAN 11

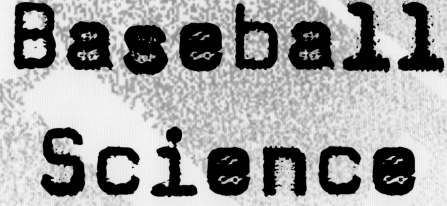

Baseball Science

James Bow

HELEN HALL LIBRARY
City of League City
100 West Walker
League City, TX 77573-3899

Crabtree Publishing Company

www.crabtreebooks.com

Crabtree Publishing Company

www.crabtreebooks.com

Author: James Bow

Editors: Molly Aloian
Leon Gray

Proofreaders: Adrianna Morganelli
Crystal Sikkens
Katherine Berti

Project coordinator: Robert Walker

Production coordinator: Margaret Amy Salter

Prepress technician: Margaret Amy Salter

Designer: Lynne Lennon

Picture researcher: Sean Hannaway

Managing editor: Tim Cooke

Art director: Jeni Child

Design manager: David Poole

Editorial director: Lindsey Lowe

Children's publisher: Anne O'Daly

Photographs:

Action Images: Hans Deryk: pages 8–9; Bill Janscha: page 9 (bottom);
Eric Miller: page 10; Steve Nesius: page 11 (bottom); Rebecca
Cook: page 18; Kimberly White: page 19; Mark Blinch: page 20;
John Sommers II: page 21 (bottom); Kim Kyung-Hoon: page 28
Alamy: Aflo Foto: page 7; Philip Scalia: page 11 (top);
David L. Moore: page 29 (bottom)
Corbis: Bettmann: page 17
Getty Images: Otto Greule Jr: pages 4–5; Mitchell Layton: page
13 (top); MLB Photos: page 23; Doug Pensinger: page 25 (right);
Mark Cunningham: page 26; Toshifumi Kitamura: page 29 (top)
PA Photos: Andrew Innerarity: page 6; John Ulan: pages 16,
21 (top), 24
Shutterstock: Joseph Gareri: front cover; Steven Pepple: page 4;
Carlos E. Santa Maria: page 9 (top); Dennis Ku: pages 12 , 13;
Paul Yates: page 14; GurganusImages: page 25 (left); Jenny
Solomon: page 27; Paul Yates: backgrounds

Illustrations:

Mark Walker: pages 17, 23

Every effort has been made to trace the owners of copyrighted material.

Library and Archives Canada Cataloguing in Publication

Bow, James, 1972-
Baseball science / James Bow.

(Sports science)
Includes index.
ISBN 978-0-7787-4534-1 (bound).--ISBN 978-0-7787-4551-8 (pbk.)

1. Baseball--Juvenile literature. 2. Sports sciences--Juvenile
literature. I. Title. II. Series: Sports science (St. Catharines, Ont.)

GV867.5.B69 2008   j796.35701'5   C2008-907026-7

Library of Congress Cataloging-in-Publication Data

Bow, James.
Baseball science / James Bow.
p. cm. -- (Sports science)
Includes index.
ISBN 978-0-7787-4551-8 (pbk. : alk. paper) -- ISBN 978-0-7787-4534-1
(reinforced library binding : alk. paper)
1. Baseball--Juvenile literature. 2. Sports sciences--Juvenile literature.
I. Title. II. Series.

GV867.5.B685 2009
796.357--dc22

2008046274

Crabtree Publishing Company

www.crabtreebooks.com   1-800-387-7650

Published in Canada
Crabtree Publishing
616 Welland Ave.
St. Catharines, Ontario
L2M 5V6

Published in the United States
Crabtree Publishing
PMB16A
350 Fifth Ave., Suite 3308
New York, NY 10118

Published in 2009 by CRABTREE PUBLISHING COMPANY.
All rights reserved. No part of this publication may be reproduced,
stored in a retrieval system or be transmitted in any form or by
any means, electronic, mechanical, photocopying, recording, or
otherwise, without the prior written permission of Crabtree
Publishing Company. In Canada: We acknowledge the financial
support of the Government of Canada through the Book Publishing
Industry Development Program (BPIDP) for our publishing
activities. © 2009 The Brown Reference Group plc.

Contents

Introducing Baseball

A pitcher and a batter face each other. The pitcher winds up and sends the ball flying toward home plate. The batter swings, there's a crack, and the ball flies through the air. Will the ball go over the fence for a **home run**? Or will a fielder pluck it from the air?

Baseball was born in the United States in the 19th century and has become the country's national sport. The sport is now played throughout the world. There are leagues in China, Cuba, Japan, Taiwan, and many other countries, including those of Latin America.

Comerica Park is home to the Detroit Tigers baseball team.

NEW WORDS

home run In major-league play, a ball hit out of the field to score a run for the batter and base runners

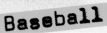

Ben Broussard of the Seattle Mariners stands ready at bat during a game against the San Diego Padres.

Rules of the game

In a game of baseball, one team's pitcher throws the ball while the players from the other team take turns trying to hit the ball with the bat. If the batter hits the ball, he or she runs past three bases set out as a diamond and heads back to home plate. Batters are safe if they reach a base, but they can only score a run if they reach home plate. The batter is out if the ball is caught without a bounce or if he or she is tagged after hitting the ball. After three outs, the teams switch sides. The game continues for nine innings per team, or until there's a winner.

Baseball science

Baseball is a sport of heroes, from the batter who hits the winning home run to the pitcher who throws the **perfect game**. Pitchers put their entire bodies into their throws, and batters hit balls moving at 100 mph (160 km/h). How do players train for a game? How do pitches change direction in midair? And why are fans obsessed with statistics?

Baseball timeline

1839	Baseball invented by Alexander Doubleday
1865	Overhand pitching allowed
1876	National League starts
1900	American League formed. World Series starts
1920	"Spitball" banned
1927	Babe Ruth hits 60 home runs
1932	Baseballs standardized
1941	Joe DiMaggio hits for 56 consecutive games
1961	Roger Maris hits 61 home runs
1998	Sammy Sosa and Marc McGuire both break in-season home run record
2007	Barry Bonds hits his 762nd home run

perfect game A game in which every batter on one team is retired without reaching a base

All About Timing

A batter has less than half a second to see a ball that has been pitched, decide whether or not to swing, and then swing the bat to make contact.

To swing the bat, the brain sends messages to the body's muscles through the nervous system. A neuron (nerve cell) carries signals at 250 mph (400 km/h). Neurons relay messages to each other across gaps called **synapses**. Each gap causes a delay of one-half of one-thousandth of a second, but hundreds of cells have to relay the message from the brain to the body.

Reflex reactions

Reflex arcs bypass this process. In a reflex arc, the body reacts to something before the brain realizes what's going on.

A pitcher winds up to deliver a fastball.

NEW WORDS

synapse A gap between the ends of nerve fibers. Nerve signals jump across synapses from neuron to neuron

⬆ *A batter has just a fraction of a second to hit the ball once it leaves the pitcher's hand.*

This is the knee-jerk reflex, which pulls your hand away when you touch something hot or sharp. Unfortunately for the batter, the bat cannot be swung on reflex. Instead, batters decide whether or not to swing based on the first few feet of the flight of a ball. The body then takes over. Some batters get

LOOK CLOSER

Test your reactions

Ask a friend to dangle a ruler above your hand. Get ready to grab the ruler but don't touch it. Tell your friend to drop the ruler within the next five seconds. When the ruler drops, catch it, and measure how far down the ruler you made the catch. This is a measure of your reaction time. The average reaction time for a human is between 0.2 and 0.25 seconds, or roughly 8–12 inches (20–30 cm) on the ruler.

▶ ▶ ▶ ▶ ▶ ▶ ▶ ▶

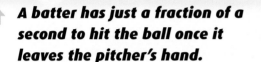

FACT! Quick fix

The best major-league pitchers pitch 100 mph (160 km/h) fastballs. The batter has just 0.4 seconds to fix on the ball, decide how it's moving, and then swing. That's just a little bit longer than it takes to blink your eyes.

into a rhythm, timing their swing to just after the pitcher throws the ball. Perfecting reaction times take years of practice. Even the best batters only get a hit three times out of ten trips to the plate.

reflex arc A nerve reaction that bypasses the brain

Hitting the Ball

A good pitch will travel from mound to home plate in less than half a second.

Batters have to think fast to hit the ball. In the first 100 **milliseconds**, the batter locks on to the pitch. In the next 125 milliseconds, the brain gauges speed and decides where to swing the bat. Finally, the brain signals to swing the bat. The batter has another 165 milliseconds to bring the bat around to where the ball should be when it crosses the plate.

All in the timing

The collision between bat and ball lasts for one-thousandth of a second. In that time, the batter delivers up to 7,920 pounds (3,600 kg) of force.

It takes just a fraction of a second for the batter's brain to decide to hit the ball.

NEW WORDS

millisecond   One-thousandth of a second

The force from the swinging bat combines with the speed of the pitch to accelerate the ball. If the ball reaches 110 mph (180 km/h), it will have the speed it needs to travel out of the park.

Sweet spot

The sweet spot is a point far enough from the batter's hands to transfer a lot of force to the ball, but not so far as to waste that energy through **vibration**. The spot is about 6⅔ inches (16.5 cm) from the end of the bat. Hitting the ball within ⅛ inch (0.3 cm) from this spot delivers the best hit.

➡ *Hank Aaron hits his 714th home run at Riverfront Stadium in Cincinnati, Ohio.*

LOOK CLOSER

Corking the bat

Some batters have been caught drilling holes in their bats and putting cork inside the holes. Not only are batters thrown out of a game for doing this, they are not helping their swing. The lighter cork absorbs more of the force of the ball, meaning that less energy is transferred back to the ball in the hit. So why do batters cork? Many just cannot let go of the mistaken idea that a lighter bat means a faster swing.

FACT! ▶▶▶▶▶▶▶

The Hammer

Hank Aaron ("the Hammer") hit at least 30 home runs in 15 different seasons. He holds major-league records for career runs batted in (2,297), bases taken (6,856), and extra base hits (1,477). His record of 755 career home runs stood for 31 years until Barry Bonds beat it in 2007.

vibration   When an object shakes very fast

Fit for the Game

Batters can hit the ball with up to 7,000 pounds (3,175 kg) of force. Pitchers toss dozens of pitches at top speed. Everyone runs bases, chases balls, and makes hard throws to get runners out.

Unlike aerobic sports such as soccer or cycling, baseball is an **anaerobic sport**. It does not raise a player's heart rate for long stretches of time. Instead, muscles act in short bursts and burn the energy quickly. The baseball season lasts from spring to fall, so endurance plays a big part in the game.

Players warm up with sprints to get blood flowing around the body and keep the muscles flexible.

▶▶▶▶▶▶▶▶ Muscle strains

FACT!

Most baseball injuries involve ligament sprains or muscle strains. These type of injuries can take a player out of the game for weeks. Pitchers are most at risk from these type of injuries.

NEW WORDS ● ● ● ● ● ● ● ●

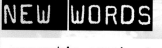

anaerobic sport A type of sport that the body can do without increasing oxygen consumption

LOOK CLOSER

Simple stretches

Try these simple stretches to stay flexible.
Knee Roll-Over Lie on your back with your arms out to the side, bend your knees, and let them fall to one side. Let your hips and back rotate with your knees.
Elbow-Out Stand and place your hand behind the middle of your back with your elbow pointing out. With your other hand, gently pull your elbow forward.
Rotating Wrist Stretch an arm straight ahead, put your palm out. With your other hand, gently pull back on the palm to stretch the wrist.

Nutrition

Baseball players need a steady flow of energy. Rather than stuffing themselves with three meals a day, they eat six smaller snacks. Their meals are high in protein (meat, fish, eggs), carbohydrates (whole grains, fruits, vegetables), and fatty acids (fish). Players should drink up to 2½ gallons (9 liters) of water per day, and over half a gallon (2.2 liters) during a game. Water eliminates toxins, helps to keep players cool, and prevents **dehydration**. Without water, players would not be able to play on a hot day.

➡ *Players should drink plenty of liquid to prevent dehydration.*

dehydration   A condition that develops when people lose more water than they are taking in

Baseball Gear

Fielders wear gloves to protect the hand and help catch the ball.

You can play baseball with very little gear—nine gloves, a bat, and a ball. As players enter the major leagues, however, the equipment gets more complex.

Gloves are made from leather. They have padding over the palm, long webbed fingers, and a pocket between the thumb and fingers. The gloves of the infielders are smaller than those of the outfielders, with a shallower pocket to help them grab the ball for a quick throw. Batters' gloves are thin but padded for grip and to absorb the shock from a hit. All the players wear shoes with cleats to grip the ground for base running or catching a flyball. Batters wear helmets with styrofoam on the ear flaps. The helmets protect the head from wild pitches.

NEW WORDS

circumference The distance around a circle or a sphere (such as a baseball)

12

LOOK CLOSER

Making baseballs

Baseballs are made by wrapping yarn around a center of cork or rubber and stitching a cowhide or horsehide cover on top. According to major league rules, baseballs must be 9 inches (23 cm) in **circumference** and weigh ⅓ of a pound (149 g).

Baseball bat

Only wooden bats are allowed in major leagues. The wood is air-dried for up to two years before being turned on a **lathe**. Bats can be no longer than 42 inches (106 cm), no more than 2¾ inches (7 cm) thick at the thickest part, and no heavier than 2⅕ pounds (1 kg).

A worker turns a piece of ash on a lathe to manufacture a baseball bat.

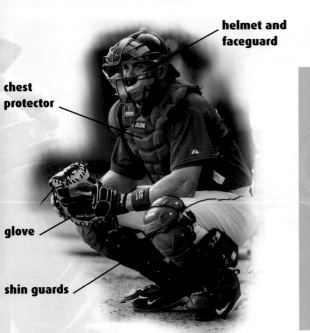

helmet and faceguard

chest protector

glove

shin guards

LOOK CLOSER

Catcher's gear

The catcher is the pitcher's true target and needs even more protection than the batter. A helmet with a faceguard protects the head and face, a chest protector covers the chest, and shin guards protect the shins. The gloves are 34 inches (86 cm) across and offer protection and a target for the pitcher. Since catchers squat behind the plate, "knee savers" attach to the calves and allow the knees to rest during breaks in the game.

lathe   A tool that can shape materials such as wood by spinning them against a cutting surface

The Windup

Professional pitchers use their whole bodies to pitch the ball. Energy from as far away as their feet is transferred to the ball to push it as fast as possible toward the batter at home plate. This is called the windup.

Pitchers stand facing sideways, with a shoulder toward home plate. They step forward, turning toward the plate, driving fast with their legs, then hips, shoulders, and arm, before throwing with their wrist and fingers. This process is called a summation of movement.

Once a pitcher has started his or her pitching motion, or windup, he or she is committed to throwing the pitch.

1.   2.

NEW WORDS

momentum   The force something has when it moves. It is the product of an object's mass and velocity (speed)

Large masses (legs and hips) move first followed by smaller ones (shoulders and arms). It's like a whip cracking from the thick handle to the tiny tip.

Taking its toll

Pitchers train for years to improve the timing of their windup so that all the **momentum** is transferred to the ball. But pitching is hard on the body. Many pitchers are forced to retire because of **arthritis** or injuries such as damaged ligaments. Of all the players on the field, a pitcher is most likely to be injured.

LOOK CLOSER

Fastest pitch

The *Guinness Book of World Records* says that Nolan Ryan (right) threw the fastest pitch—a 100.9 mph (162.4 km/h) fastball in 1974. Joel Zumaya pitched at 104 mph (167.4 km/h) in 2006, but the radar guns used to measure the pitch may have been faulty. Some say that Steve Dalkowski had the fastest pitch at up to 110 mph (177 km/h). He did not play in the majors. He could not control his pitches.

3.

4.

5.

arthritis Inflammation of the joints, which is accompanied by pain, stiffness, and swelling

The Perfect Pitch

Throwing a fastball is not enough to force a strike. In his best year, Roger Clemens, one of the best fastball pitchers, gave up 151 hits and lost eight games.

The pitcher's arsenal includes other throws that do not depend entirely on speed. Curveballs move away or toward the batter. Sliders dip down in the last few feet. Knuckleballs move erratically.

The pitcher tries to throw the ball so that the batter cannot hit it.

NEW WORDS

vortex   A spiral of air or water, similar to a tornado or a whirlpool

All about forces

Air resistance is the key to throwing sneaky pitches. A moving ball pushes the air in front of it aside. Air crashes in behind the ball, creating a **vortex** that trails the ball like a comet's tail. When the ball is spinning, the tail can point slightly up, down, or side to side. The force of the vortex on the ball is known as the Magnus effect. The air passing over the side of the ball without a vortex catches the ball and presses on it. This pushes the ball to one side, making it curve through the air or drop suddenly, fooling the batter.

FACT! ▶▶▶▶▶▶▶▶

Pitching hall of fame

Cy Young (played 1890–1911): Set many pitching records that stood for a century. Most career wins (511).

Sandy Koufax (1955–1966): His curveball won him 165 games and four no-hitters (second highest career record).

Hoyt Wilhelm (1952–1972): Knuckleball helped him save 200 games.

Randy Johnson (1988–): His late-diving 87 mph (140 km/h) slider fools batters into thinking they have a fastball.

Pedro Martinez (1992–): Devastating **changeup** is just one of the pitches that keeps the batters guessing.

LOOK CLOSER

Grip to pitch

Curveball Grip ball with middle and index fingers where the seams are closest together. Throw ball, rolling it off index finger while spinning it with thumb and middle finger.

Knuckleball Press index, middle, and ring fingers on the seam and the thumb on the bottom. Keep wrist straight and pitch with fingers extended toward home plate.

Slider Grip ball with middle and index fingers across the widest two seams, and slightly off-center with ring and pinky finger off to the side. Throw like a fastball, and have ball roll off index finger.

Changeup Center index, middle, and ring fingers where the seams are widest apart. Tuck thumb and pinky below ball. Throw with stiff wrist like a fastball.

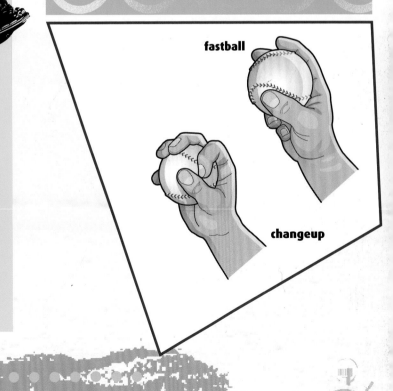

fastball

changeup

changeup A slow pitch that is used to confuse a batter who is expecting a faster pitch

Out of the Park

The batter swings and the bat connects with the ball. But will it be a home run or just a flyball caught for an easy out? From the moment of impact, different forces work together to prevent the batter from scoring a run.

As soon as the bat makes contact with the ball, both the bat and ball deform. This wastes energy in the same way that shock absorbers waste away energy as an automobile drives over a pothole. Then there is the force of gravity. A ball flying through the air is a **projectile**. The ball is pulled down by the force of gravity at a rate of 33 feet (10 m) per second. A baseball must travel at a certain upward angle to counter the pull of gravity and clear the fence. Hit the ball too high, and it stays in the air for a long time but does not travel very far, resulting in a "fly out." Hit the ball too low, and it shoots forward, but hits the ground much too early.

A ball clears the outstretched hand of an outfielder and sails over the fence for a home run.

NEW WORDS

projectile Any object that travels through the air under the force of gravity

Batters do not always aim for the fence. If the wind is blowing in from the outfield, it can turn home runs into deep flyballs. The batter might decide to keep the angle low, blasting the ball between the fielders for a base hit.

Something in the air

The air also works against the batter. A ball hit in the thin air of Denver—one mile (1.6 km) above sea level—will travel 36 feet (11 m) farther than the same ball, hit by the same bat, in the dense, humid air of a ballpark at sea level. The Colorado Rockies started to store their baseballs in humidors when they found that the dry air of Denver dried out the balls.

Barry Bonds tops the career home run leaderboard.

LOOK CLOSER

Hitting angles

In a **vacuum**, the best angle to fight gravity and get a ball to travel as far as possible is a 45-degree angle. The ball travels forward as fast as it travels up. Add air to the mix, and you need more forward speed to fight the drag. To clear the ballpark, the batter hopes to hit the ball so it leaves the bat at 130 mph (210 km/h) at a 35-degree angle from the ground.
Try it for yourself, varying hitting speeds and angles, at this website: http://whyfiles.org/152baseball/2.html

When bats hit these balls, the balls did not squash as much as they would in other, more humid cities. More energy from the bat was transferred to the ball, making home runs easier to hit. Changes to the rules mean that all the game balls are now stored in humidors to ensure the same types of balls are hit, regardless of the ballpark.

vacuum An enclosed space empty of air

Fielding the Ball

Beyond the pitcher, eight other players take the field, helping the pitcher's team keep the score down.

The catcher guards home plate and tags out runners racing home.

Players at the bases are good at **tagging out** runners if the fielders throw the ball in time. The catcher catches pitches that go by the batter and stays alert for anybody stealing second or third base. The left, center, and right outfielders catch flyballs, grab line drives, and throw to the correct basemen to tag runners out. The shortstop guards the inner outfield. Infielders have just a fraction of a second to field the ball before it passes by. The fielders stand ready, shifting from side to side without moving their feet, waiting to spring into action.

Catching the ball

When a flyball sails into the air, the outfielder runs to where he or she thinks the ball might land. The outfielder keeps the ball in his or her **field of vision.**

NEW WORDS

tagging out When a fielder touches a base runner while holding a live ball, thus putting him out of play

LOOK CLOSER

The "hot corner"

Third base is known as the "hot corner" because the third baseman is close to the batter and most right-handed batters tend to hit the ball toward third base. The third baseman must be quick and have good hand-eye coordination to catch hard line drives.

➡ *An outfielder runs to catch a flyball.*

Balls hit directly to the outfielder are harder to catch. It takes a couple of seconds before an outfielder can see where the ball is curving and judge where it will land. An outfielder can watch the batter's swing and listen for the crack as it hits the ball. The outfielder has less than four seconds to race to where the ball will land and place his or her glove beneath it. Scientists have built robots that can predict where a flyball will land, but catching the ball is still too complicated for robots to master.

▶ ▶ ▶ ▶ ▶ ▶ ▶ ▶

FACT!

All-rounder

Center fielder Willie Mays has the most putouts by an outfielder (catching flies and tagging runners off base), with 7,095 in 22 seasons. With 660 home runs and 3,283 hits, he was one of the best players in the sport.

field of vision The area that a person can see without moving his or her eyes or head

21

Baseball Park

The first baseball parks were open fields. When stands were built to hold people paying to see the games, ballparks became varied and complicated stadiums.

The diamond gets its name from the four bases laid out in a 90-foot (27-m) diamond, with the pitcher's mound in the middle. The outfield is less rigid. Foul lines extend from home plate through first and third bases to the fence. Balls hit between these lines are fair. The fence can be up to 355 feet (108 m) from home plate along the foul lines, and up to 435 feet (132 m) in center field. Some short fields stop "cheap" home runs with walls to box them in. The Green Monster is the 37-foot (11-m) wall in Boston's Fenway Park.

Whatever the weather

Baseball is a summer sport, and fans love to watch it in the open air.

Houston Astrodome is a domed ballpark with artificial turf.

NEW WORDS

retractable   Capable of being drawn or pulled back

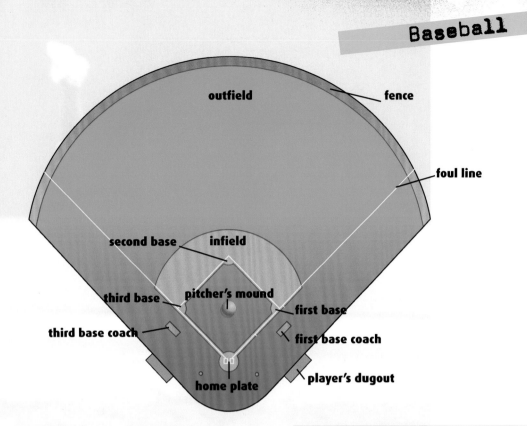

outfield

fence

foul line

second base · infield

third base · pitcher's mound

first base

third base coach

first base coach

player's dugout

home plate

⬆ *This illustration shows the main features of a typical ballpark.*

Games have been cancelled because of rain, causing ballpark designers to look at ways to keep the field dry. Domed stadiums appeared in the 1960s thanks to new construction methods that put a **retractable** roof over the field. Many ballparks now use artificial turf, because it saves on groundwork and can be used where grass cannot grow. First used at the Houston Astrodome in 1964, giving one brand the name *astroturf,* this carpet of plastic grass has evolved.

LOOK CLOSER

Retractable roofs

The roofs of domed stadiums cover a vast area. It is a real engineering challenge to make them open and close. Toronto's massive domed roof comes apart in three sections, two of which pull over a hotel located north of the field, and another of which rotates out of the way. These sections move on railroad tracks.

Artificial grass has more natural-looking **synthetic** fibers and rubber infill so that the surface has more give for players running and sliding along the ground.

synthetic Something that is produced by people and not found in nature

Baseball Tactics

Baseball is a tense, psychological game. A pitcher who loses his or her cool could walk the batter. A batter who swings too fast will strike out. Fielders who drop balls change an out into a base hit.

Baseball is a team game that relies on cooperation between players.

During a game, the batter tries to guess what pitch will come next and the pitcher tries not to give away any clues. Fielders try to guess whether a batter will hit the ball deep or shallow. When a batter gets on base, he or she may try to "steal" the next base by running for it as the pitcher throws to the next batter. A player can be caught stealing a base if he or she does not run fast enough or moves too soon or too late.

Hitting to win

Batters try to hit fielders out of position and allow runners on base to score. The sacrifice fly is a long, high ball hit deep into the outfield.

NEW WORDS

bunt   Hitting the ball lightly without swinging the bat

Catchers "speak" to pitchers and infielders using hand signals.

LOOK CLOSER

Take a walk!

In 1920, rule changes led to a rise in hits and home runs. Before the rule changes, one ball was used for the entire game, and foul balls were thrown back onto the field and reused. Fielders could scuff the ball and give their pitchers an advantage. In the modern game, the balls are replaced at the first sign of wear, making them brighter and easier for the batter to see.

The sacrifice fly puts the outfielders well back and gives a runner time to tag his or her base and dash for second, third, or even home. When batters **bunt**, they tap the ball with their bat rather than swing at it, knocking it into the dirt in front of them. This pulls the infielders closer, giving runners on base time to run.

Pitchers hide their grip on the ball during the windup so batters cannot guess the pitch.

Keep concentrating

Concentration is equally as important as strength and speed. Many pitchers are more likely to throw strikes if they have had a run of throwing strikes. It's when the streak ends that the pressure is on. The best baseball players can overcome any blows to their **confidence**.

confidence   Belief in yourself and your abilities

Stat Attack!

The Major League has been keeping track of baseball statistics since the middle of the 19th century. Players, managers, and fans pore over these figures to try and get a deeper understanding of the game.

The term *sabermetrics* comes from SABR, which stands for Society for American Baseball Research. Sabermetrics use the statistics from baseball games to compare players and test **hypotheses**.

↑ *A spectator keeps score during a game.*

Calculating averages

Number of home runs hit by A. Batter from 2001 to 2009

Year	2001	2002	2003	2004	2005	2006	2007	2008	2009
Home runs	22	9	21	22	18	19	22	16	22

Mean: Take x measurements, add them, and divide by x. From the statistics above, the batter has a mean of 171/9 = 19 home runs a year.

Median: Rank your x measurements in order and select the one measurement in the middle. From the statistics above, the batter has a median of 21 home runs a year: 9, 16, 18, 19, **21**, 22, 22, 22, 22.

Mode: The result that appears most often in a set of measurements. From the statistics above, the batter has a mode of 22 home runs a year.

NEW WORDS

hypotheses   Predictions that can be tested through further research

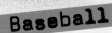

For example, is pitching more important than hitting? Just use the statistics to compare teams with the best pitching statistics against teams with the best hitting statistics to see who won more games.

Simple stats

Batting average is calculated by the number of hits (home runs or other times the batter gets on base after hitting a ball) for each time at bat. The earned run average counts the runs scored against a pitcher (except for those that happen due to another player's error, like a dropped flyball). It is calculated by runs scored divided by innings played multiplied by nine. Runs batted in (RBIs) count the number of runs each batter scores with any hit, home run, or sacrifice fly.

What's the point?

Scouts and managers use sabermetrics to decide how to draft or trade players or to figure out the **strategy** during a game. Is a pitcher better against right-handed batters than left-handed ones? That pitcher might then find a lot of left-handed batters substituted into the game.

LOOK CLOSER

The Triple Crown

The Triple Crown of pitching belongs to the pitcher who, at season's end, has the best Earned Run Average, the most wins, and the most strikeouts. Jake Peavy won this while playing for the San Diego Padres in 2007.
The Triple Crown of batting belongs to the hitter who, at season's end, has the most home runs, most runs batted in, and the best batting average. This was last held by Carl Yastrzemski of the Boston Red Sox in 1967.

The scoreboard summarizes the state of play.

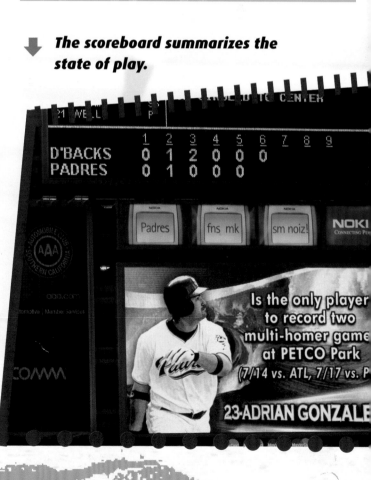

The Future of Baseball

Baseball is nearly 170 years old, and the sport is still full of tradition. But advances in technology are changing the way the game is played.

Cameras are getting smaller and lighter and may find themselves on the front of a player's baseball cap, or even on the ball. New training techniques and better nutrition are helping the body play with greater consistency and for much longer. This allows players to extend their careers. Some people think that players will be hitting 50 hits well after the age of 50, and that Barry Bond's career record of 762 home runs will be broken sooner rather than later.

LOOK CLOSER

World sport

Major-league baseball has only one team operating outside the United States (the Toronto Blue Jays from Canada), but the sport's popularity is growing across the world. Major-league baseball has scheduled exhibition and regular series games in China, Japan, and Mexico. As new leagues open up, full-time teams may be set up in cities in Latin America and Asia. Spectators may finally get a World Series that lives up to its name.

NEW WORDS

specialize   To focus on a particular skill or ability

LOOK CLOSER

Changing the rules

When the American League brought in the **designated hitter** (DH) so that pitchers did not have to bat, fans reacted angrily. The American League continues to play with the DH, but the National League does not. Even with the DH controversy, the drive for better hitters and fielders may force teams to **specialize** and set up hitting and fielding squads for games.

Computer games offer simulations of the real game.

Sony's robot, QR10, pitches like a real baseball pitcher.

New technologies

Will people ever play against robots? Scientists have figured out how to make a robot move to where a flyball will land. Now they have to figure out how to make it catch the ball. Some modern ballparks are designed to recall the golden age of baseball, but with advances such as climate control, domed roofs, and television screens to show the action in the field.

designated hitter (DH) A player who bats in place of the pitcher in the batting order

Glossary

anaerobic sport A type of sport that the body can do without increasing oxygen consumption

arthritis Inflammation of the joints, which is accompanied by pain, stiffness, and swelling

bunt Hitting the ball lightly without swinging the bat

changeup A slow pitch that is used to confuse a batter who is expecting a faster pitch

circumference The distance around a circle or a sphere (such as a baseball)

confidence Belief in yourself and your abilities

dehydration A condition that develops when people lose more water than they are taking in

designated hitter (DH) A player who bats in place of the pitcher in the batting order

field of vision The area that a person can see without moving his or her eyes or head

home run In major-league play, a ball hit out of the field to score a run for the batter and base runners

hypotheses Predictions that can be tested through further research

lathe A tool that can shape materials such as wood by spinning them against a cutting surface

millisecond One-thousandth of a second

momentum The force something has when it moves. It is the product of an object's mass and velocity (speed)

perfect game A game in which every batter on one team is retired without reaching a base

projectile Any object that travels through the air under the force of gravity

reflex arc A nerve reaction that bypasses the brain

retractable Capable of being drawn or pulled back

specialize To focus on a particular skill or ability

strategy A plan of action to gain advantage over the opposing team and win the game

synapse A gap between the ends of nerve fibers. Nerve signals jump across synapses from neuron to neuron

synthetic Something that is produced by people and not found in nature

tagging out When a fielder touches a base runner while holding a live ball, thus putting him out of play

vacuum An enclosed space empty of air

vibration When an object shakes very fast

vortex A spiral of air or water, similar to a tornado or a whirlpool

Find Out More

Books

Baseball (DK Eyewitness Books). Editors of DK Publishing. New York: DK Children, 2005.

Fridell, Ron. *Sports Technology (Cool Science)*. Minneapolis, Minnesota: Lerner Publications, 2008.

Goodstein, Madeline. *Sports Science Projects: The Physics of Balls in Motion*. Berkeley Heights, New Jersey: Enslow Publishers, 1999.

Jacobs, Greg. *Everything Kids' Baseball Book*. Cincinnati, Ohio: Adams Media, 2008.

Jennison, Christopher. *Baseball Math*. Tucson, Arizona: Good Year Books, 2006.

Thomas, Keltie. *How Baseball Works*. Toronto, Ontario: Maple Tree Press, 2008.

Web sites

The How Stuff Works website explains everything you need to know about baseball, from the equipment and rules to the organization of the major leagues.

http://entertainment.howstuffworks.com/baseball.htm

Find out what helps a curveball bend as it moves through the air and how the atmosphere can help you hit a home run at the Why Files website.

http://whyfiles.org/152baseball/

San Francisco's Exploratorium website explores the science behind baseball. The site includes some excellent animations that will test your reaction time and find out what it takes to hit a home run.

http://www.exploratorium.edu/baseball/

Index

Printed in the U.S.A. – BG